Contents:

First published in 2005 by The School of Emotional Literacy

This edition published in 2008 by Speechmark Publishing Ltd,
70 Alston Drive, Bradwell Abbey, Milton Keynes MK13 9HG
Tel: +44 (0) 1908 326944   Fax: +44 (0) 1908 326960

www.speechmark.net
www.schoolofemotional-literacy.com

British Library Cataloguing in Publication Data
A catalogue record for this book is available from the British Library

002-5539 / Printed in the United Kingdom / 3080

ISBN: 978 086388 742 0

Acknowledgements

My particular acknowledgement in this Workbook is to Hampstead School, which has given me the opportunity to develop a Counselling Practice for the school and to join with the school in the promotion of further Emotional Literacy, in an already emotionally literate school. Indeed, a school with such understanding of Inclusion that the Headteacher was asked to permit OFSTED the opportunity to make a training film of the work of the Inclusion Teams.

I would like also to mention Dr. Elizabeth Morris, Principal of the School of Emotional Literacy, without whose continued inspiration I would have been less adventurous; also Heather Daulphin, Senior Deputy at Hampstead School who has been the co-trainer with me in delivering my course. She has offered illustration of such immediate relevance between the course and the needs of the school. I am indebted too to Rachel Carter, the Publishing Manager of the School of Emotional Literacy, who continuously offers invaluable help and encouragement in the preparation for publication.

I am indebted to Sarah Vinnels for her permission to include her poem "Alone" in the course material. Similarly, I am indebted to Christian Aid for their permission to include their telling advertisement "What kind of child does this to her doll?" I also thank Elizabeth Morris for so freely permitting use of her Emotional Literacy materials.

Author's Introduction

In 2004, when writing "Establishing a Counselling Service in Your School" I wrote that "School's are organic institutions and both endogenous and exogenous shocks to the system make constant revision of ideas necessary". This means that now I see the need to revise last year's Workbook and also to prepare this one.

This current volume, like the earlier one, has grown out of the enthusiasm from the people with whom I work. The 2004 Workbook, and its current revision, was driven by the enthusiasm of the student trainees of Peer Buddying, both to learn and to wish to offer help to their peers. The new Workbook arises from numerous enquiries from staff, both about what I do (and how I do it) and how they may work with a greater grasp of Emotional Literacy in their encounters with students and colleagues.

It has been a pleasure to put together courses both for the students and the staff and it has been hugely enlightening for me to design courses, which embrace "what is going on" for the school. In my practice, with my schoolwork and with my private clients, I have always paid particular attention to Phenomenology in that work. That is what demands the need to be particularly up-to-date, not only with the latest research that may have relevance, but especially to the "here and now" of the staff and students.

Part of the "here and now" was the coincidence of my thoughts about the staff course set out in this book and the Behavioural Audit which the school engaged in. So I researched staff enthusiasm for the course in that context, using that context also as a guide for the content. It was also in the context of a national "here and now". There was a press release in April 2004 from the Journal of Counselling in Education (BACP) quoting Margaret Hodge, then Secretary of State for Education & Skills:
"............Strong emotional health is vital to every child and adult alike...... young people, particularly in adolescence, can feel that they are living through a nightmare......all too often it seems that there is no-one to talk to......The ethos of the school is key, not only to the academic achievements of its young people, but also to the well-being of both staff and students. It seems to me that a whole school approach based upon mutual respect must represent the way forward......"

The school for which I designed the course has that core belief of the "Whole school approach" with its motto of "Learning together, Achieving together".

Of further relevance to the "here and now" of any secondary school is its size and, therefore, whilst a significant proportion of the staff may have been involved in Counselling and Emotional Literacy developments in the school, there will be staff for whom these developments are not as completely known as would be optimal for the emotional health of the school population. Furthermore, as in any large school the numbers involved in staff turnover will be significant.

2 The Programme

In outline the shape of the programme of this Staff Foundation Course is not dissimilar to the Peer Buddying Course I deliver to students. However, its content is more demanding and shaped very much by embracing ideas from colleagues, both about delivery and content. Indeed, it gains much of its relevance from the huge wealth of Continuing Professional Development that today is seen as sine qua non in the Teaching and Therapy professions. It is also designed to encourage the wish to study more deeply – it is only an introduction.

The module order and content are designed to embrace student well-being as well as staff emotional literacy. It starts with those elements that would be "key" in any psycho-therapeutic context and in discussion would hopefully be a paradigm for the classroom for the teachers involved. Material for the modules are best produced on single sheets and handed to course members in the order and at the time that it is introduced in the training. In every cohort to date I have delivered this as a bi-weekly training, both to give the staff time to absorb the material and also not to overload them, in what is always a busy schedule of post-school meetings for teaching staff. Co-incidentally, this also permits the course to fit into those schools, which practise a bi-weekly time-table.

Module 1
In module one, as in all eight modules, it is helpful both to the trainer and the trainee to have a checklist at the outset of the module. So amongst the photo-copiable material are a series of checklists, to stand as they are, or to be a model from which your own may vary. It is a means of identifying what is the content of the module without having to rummage through all the papers. In module one it also serves as a means of listing introductory concepts and approaches that will be relevant and present throughout the course. My aim in providing so many sheets to be handed out is to make it unnecessary for the course participants to have to take any notes. The course is, above all else, an experiential one.

Thus the checklist for module one starts with the introductory concept of equality – which can be full of impact in schools, which are at the very least organisationally hierarchical. So one of the first things I remind staff about is my use of two identical chairs in my Counselling Room and my use of my first name in my work with students. I remind them of this both to explain my work (I work from a Humanistic stance) and also because it relates to the ideal of equality of feeling between students and the Counsellor in the classroom. It was an especially mixed cohort of staff when first I delivered this course. It contained almost every level of hierarchy in a school of 150 staff. This had both positive and negative potential and was wonderfully illustrative of our various "takes" on the issue of equality.

When I designed this course it was to coincide with the school's Behavioural Audit and one very useful piece of work was the handout for a staff meeting on student behaviour at the outset of the audit. A clear indicator of the school's already emotionally literate approach was the production of this discussion sheet with the following headings:
Issues conspiring against us – difficult for us to do anything about
e.g. the disruption from the building of a new floor on the front school block.
Issues conspiring against us – thing we could change
e.g. poor quality environment in certain areas.
New systems put in place – new systems we should put in place
This was a list from an emotionally literate management team not so "defensive" that it would not openly discuss issues that may invite discomfort. I included this sheet (a different one could be included for your own institution) to illustrate the relevance of an emotionally literate "culture" at the outset of the course.

Fundamental to running any group is Group Rules and, for the purposes of such a course as this, the rules simply have to include acceptance of confidentiality about all participant contributions.

The checklist for module one then becomes one of content – as for the succeeding seven modules. In the first session there is need for an explanation of Group Process as distinct from Content. For some who may have experience of Circle Time in Primary Schools this is more easy to understand. Indeed there are many teachers who have undertaken some counselling skills training and are already aware of the concept. For those for whom it is a new concept then a good way to start is for the trainer(s) to begin input with their own Process after indicating that this will be the starting point of all the modules.

One of my memories from undertaking a post-graduate Psychosexual Therapy and Human Relations course at The London Institute of Human Sexuality is when we were introduced to a weekend of films and training in human behaviours, which were not familiar to us. At the outset of a modest introductory course such bombardment of experience would be inappropriate. However, it can be valuable to know something of the intensity of feeling a client may bring to a counselling room. With this in mind I introduced the staff to a dark poem written by a poet known to me.

Immediately following comment upon that poem and from what it may have emerged, I issue notes on Confidentiality. The most helpful publication that I can recommend on this area is "Working with Young People" from Essex University's Children's Legal Centre. One of the experiences most valued by young people that I have seen over the years has been the degree of confidentiality that is possible. It is useful for classroom teachers to remind themselves that some students feel that there is low level of confidentiality offered to them when talking to teachers, not least because of what gets back to parents in Consultation Evenings and the like. A very useful discussion can take place over this and the comparative advantage that a counsellor has over the teacher in this regard.

The questionnaire that follows in the contents list for module one, is one designed by the School of Emotional Literacy. Whilst I deliberately separate the completion of the questionnaire from a formal interpretation of it (to be done in the succeeding module) it is a fascinating exercise to see the reaction of staff to it and their amazement as to how it appears to "classify" them. Again, it is an interesting model for remembering how pupils in the classroom want to talk about the work that they are set.

The final sheets handed out in module one are self-analysis sheets copied from my Peer Buddy course – which are useful for future discussion as to whether staff choose to complete them, module by module, or not. I offer it as a means of participants being able to monitor their own degree of involvement and their growing awareness of their feelings about their and others' involvement. They may choose to explain the stance they took at the final module or in their evaluation forms offered on completion of the course.

Module 2

Module two should begin with a reminder of group rules, especially confidentiality. I remember a colleague making particular use of this in a wonderfully brave contribution to Group Process, the next piece of content in module two.

In order to remain as topical and relevant to the particular school, illustration from a current document or incident may be appropriate as in module one. In the first delivery of the course at Hampstead School, I remember taking a copy of the Staff Bulletin for that particular week. On the reverse side of the Bulletin there is always a Thought for the Week. On this particular week there was a poem from William Arthur Ward, listing "The Aspects of life", ending: "..............the beauty of life is to give." I chose to add: "and to receive", inviting the staff to make their own changes.

This particular module is more didactic than the other modules and contains an introduction to TA (Transactional Analysis) theory – partly because I use some of this theory in my thinking about work and partly because it a most useful approach for teachers when thinking about their "transactions" in class.

I choose to return at the end of this module to the Conditions of Worth questionnaire completed a fortnight before, both because of its relevance after some TA input and because participants are curious and deserving to know the possible origins, explanations and depth of significance of their arrived at "Drivers".

Module 3

Like all modules, three starts with Process – now at a point where it no longer needs explaining or justifying and where it is now more appropriate for the trainer(s) to contribute to Process during or when the course participants have had the opportunity to let the others know "what is going on for them".

By the time we reach module three, staff members are also more ready to receive a demonstration counselling session. I was fortunate that my co-trainer is familiar (as indeed are many teachers) with counselling and was therefore comfortable to play the role of Client in a demonstration session. Demonstration remains central to this introductory course and, from the evaluation forms is a valued part of the course, most particularly in observing a concentration upon really "hearing" the client – both spoken and unspoken "dialogue".

I provide a sheet to invite various approaches to look for during the counselling demonstration. Then I invite questions about the session – but ONLY to ask the CLIENT how they feel. Most questions should be addressed to the COUNSELLOR. Hopefully this guides staff to see that an important piece of learning is not to enquire about what goes on in the counselling session of the client and certainly not to enquire about the content of the dialogue.

Following this I introduce the course members to a picture I use in the earlier workbook "Establishing a Counselling Service in Your School". I deliberately set up a St. Trinians-like scene with some students with some bizarre behaviour. Most staff do realise that a frozen snapshot does not tell us who really may benefit from some counselling; rather that only intimate contact will reveal the needs of some.

When there has been time for a discussion of what might appropriately be dealt with in the counselling room, I explain then two confidential record sheets that I have designed and use: a Client Assessment Sheet for session one and a Client Pro Forma for each succeeding session – why I have them in that particular format.

During the school year, usually near the end – after the summer half-term – when Years 11, 12 (for a brief period) and 13 are on exam leave and, therefore, I have spare time rather than a Waiting List, I do a piece of analysis of the year's work for the school to have statistics to inform its appraisal of the Counselling Service. This is useful for the course participants to see that the counsellor is accountable.

This module is brought to a close with a more sophisticated piece of theory which follows from the earlier introduction to the theory of Transactional Analysis. This piece of theory is the Drama Triangle of Karpman (1968) and the extension to that theory from the Beneficial Triangle from unpublished work by J. Hunt, made accessible by Brigid Proctor. It is of particular help to teachers to make them aware that they are frequently being invited to enter a Drama Triangle and that they may save themselves and the pupil from the Expected Disappointment by inviting the pupil into thinking and behaviour that could lead to the Hoped for Outcome. I have deliberately put the two triangles together and left space for the course participants to fill in the Victim/Rescuer/Persecutor and Vulnerable/Responsible/Powerful labels for themselves. Inviting the course members to complete the diagrams is both a means of reinforcing this learning and as always is a paradigm for effective learning that takes place in the classroom.

Module 4

Following on from Process this is a module that is a brief introduction to Emotional Literacy and Howard Gardner's idea of Multiple Intelligence. As with all the modules of this course this is a very brief introduction and some evaluation forms make it clear that some staff would like these explanations to go further. The problem is finding enough twilight sessions that are accessible for the staff members who are most likely to be amongst those who already have significant commitment to after-school work. I spend some time in the closing module, therefore, making sure that those interested know where they can pursue further study – both Counselling Skills and Emotional Literacy.

An excellent introduction to Multiple Intelligence is a questionnaire and one such questionnaire is printed by the Network Educational Press from Smith, Alistair (1998) Accelerated Learning in Practice (pp 187/189). Dr. Elizabeth Morris offers a definition of Emotional Literacy and sets out the Principles in a very helpful list. Howard Gardner's Multiple Intelligences are defined and explained in his 1993 publication.

As I was fortunate enough to have Heather Daulphin co-presenting the first presentation of my course, she has kindly permitted me to include the sheets which she drafted to show the clear relevance to Hampstead School of twelve staff completing the Certificate Course of the School of Emotional Literacy (three of those staff have already gone on to publish work directly related to the course).

Module 5

There has been some fantastic work done in Brain Research in recent years and we can now often identify a physiological explanation for behaviour when earlier therapy had to rely on talking to and observing clients in sessions to identify explanations. I, therefore, follow the Process of this module with a diagram of the brain to outline some of what we now know from that recent research – about the impact of hormones like dopamine, serotonin and adrenalin. There have been some very helpful articles on the impact of such hormones and how we may school ourselves to change feelings and behaviour. I refer to such articles as those by Sue Gerhardt and Babette Rothschild in the BACP Journal of November 2004.

This introduction to the physiology and chemistry of the human brain leads brilliantly into Group theory and I use some of Elizabeth Morris' work to explain the justification of removing a child from the classroom to one-to-one situations. A good illustration of this is the child showing classic symptoms of adrenalin flooding the frontal part of the brain leading to an inability to think clearly and therefore leading to "Emotional Highjack". The stress of the group situation can be quickly relieved by one-to-one attention and strategies developed to invite behaviour more conducive to learning. It is likely in talking about Group Theory that individual instances (many shared ones) will occur and it can be useful to invite non-naming of those particular pupils as part of the emotionally literate approach.

Module 6

At the outset of this module I break my rule of starting with Process by handing out a sheet headed "Statement for delivery at final ("Goodbye") session. I break the rule, explaining to the course members that it may well promote feelings which could well be beneficial to explore in Process. I introduce this in module six, so that the course members have plenty of time to prepare. I also offer the opportunity not to do it, inviting that they allow themselves to experience that this is a choice they've freely made and at least letting themselves know why they have made that choice.

The importance of the exercise for me (which I also make explicit) is that it is again a model for the importance of acknowledging endings with pupils too. Too many schools permit years and school careers to end with little or no opportunity for healthy endings of Celebration and Mourning.

The main teaching focus of the module is the "Core Conditions" of Carl Rogers – with particular reference to the "Lost" conditions referred to by Keith Tudor in his BACP Journal (11/1) article of February 2000. The terminology requires explaining, though the core concepts are frequently not unfamiliar to teachers, many of whom have some acquaintance with counselling.

The other part of the module is a further counselling demonstration and, because of the fact that this is module six, the participants are better able to question the counsellor on why they did or did not say/demonstrate what is on the questioner's mind.

Module 7

Following Process I offer a sample Egogram, relevant because of the earlier module on TA, then I invite the participants to pair up for drawing their own current and wished for Egograms. Again I invite group/pair work to draw attention to the feelings of the pupils in the classroom when asked to work with others. I also make a quick reference to Franklin Ernst's OK Corrall which I then follow up in Module 8.

The most important slice of time in this module is a review of what we have done over the preceding modules and time for questions on that past work together. As in module six I refer to the next (final) module in the same way that classroom teachers would prepare their students for endings – that they may be handled optimally.

Module 8

As an emotionally literate ending this is both a combination of review and forward looking. After Process I show the celebrated Gloria recording in which a number of psychotherapists demonstrate a counselling session with the same client – Gloria. I only show the Carl Rogers recording as the others are approaches that I do not use and have not demonstrated.

Another piece of review came to mind when I saw a Christian Aid appeal in the Sunday Times at the end of the year in 2004. They have kindly given me permission to use this illustration in this publication. I have shown it in the delivery of the staff course as a way of recalling the OK Corrall and asking which quadrant they would put the girl in question in the OK Corrall. I can think of no more telling illustration.

The review takes the form of the prepared paragraph or extempore delivery from each student who feels comfortable to take part. The looking forward takes the form of giving reading information and information of Emotional Literacy courses and Therapy Institutes where counselling training is available.

There are two further forms that are important. The first is an Evaluation form – necessary for any delivery to be appraised and modified. The second is a Certificate of Attendance, especially important as an acknowledgement of achievement and also for staff folders for their CPD.

Course Modules

Module One – Confidentiality & Conditions of Worth
- Process and Content
- Handout of initial sheets including checklist and confidentiality notes
- Poem
- Conditions of Worth
- Self-awareness and self-analysis sheets

Module Two – Introduction to Transactional Analysis
- Process
- Checklist
- Some TA theory – a theoretical approach of particular relevance to the classroom
- Behavioural clues too Drivers

Module Three – Potential counselling clients and issues
- Process
- Checklist
- Demonstration counselling session
- Who needs counselling here?
- Confidential pro forma and analysis sheets used by counsellor
- Drama & Beneficial Triangles

Module Four – Emotional Literacy & Multiple Intelligence
- Process
- Emotional Literacy definition, principles and applications
- Multiple Intelligence

Module Five – Individuals and groups
- Process
- Checklist
- Human Brain
- Stages of group membership
- Group Diagrams
- What needs to happen in groups?

Module Six – Person Centred Counselling
- Process
- Checklist
- The Core Conditions of Carl Rogers
- Rogers Stages of Growth
- Demonstration counselling session
- Statement for delivery at final session – session 8

Module Seven – Our own Egograms
- Process
- Checklist
- Egograms in pairs
- The OK Corrall
- Review and preparation for the last session

Module Eight – An Emotionally Literate Goodbye
- Process
- Checklist
- Where would you place this in the OK Corrall?
- Paragraph deliveries and responses
- Sources and further reading
- Evaluation sheets
- Certificates

3

Module 1

Checklist

Introductory points:	• Equality – in all Humanistic counselling work there is a starting point of equality – so there is **no hierarchy** in this group
	• Course material - new material will be issued at each module, accompanying the module content sheet. It would be helpful to bring the file to each module
	• Group rules – these are normal **therapy group rules**
	• 8 fortnightly sessions – therefore please enter the dates in your diaries now

Module content:	1. Process – as distinct from Content
	2. Poem – "Alone"
	3. Significance of Confidentiality
	4. Questionnaire – please enter your first thoughts, not reasoned-out answers
	5. Self-analysis sheets – as with the questionnaire this is **for your eyes only, unless you wish to share information**

Staff Meetings on Student Behaviour

Issues conspiring against us (difficult for us to do anything about)
Abnormal end of the summer term
One Year out at a time for several weeks
Constant room changes
Staff resources not in correct place
Contractors on site (compounds, equipment, noise, dirt etc)
Bromcom down
ICT system disrupted
Negative external influences (poor media models etc)
Phone system disrupted
Students who see violence as acceptable (family influence)
Changing student cohort
Poor quality environment

Issues conspiring against us (things we could change)
Heads of Year that do not stay with Year throughout school
Inconsistency of approach
Agreed systems not being used by all
Inappropriate curriculum offer for some
Duties not always carried out
Poor quality environment in certain areas
Low-level disruption not challenged in some classrooms
Lack of use of baseline data/differentiation in some areas
Lack of enforcement of agreed rules by some staff (hats and coats in lessons, lack of formal registration etc
Development of blame culture

New systems put in place
Withdrawal room
Learning support unit
Increased patrols
DFES behaviour and attendance audit

New systems we should put in place

Alone

Alone in her head
With the thoughts that destroy her
Full of self-hatred for the person she is
And there is no escape
She has no one to talk to
Just the voice in her head that says there's no point

Alone in her house
Just the TV for friendship
Longing to share one of those fantasy worlds
And the phone never rings
Though the mobile's beside her
Living her life through the television shows

Alone at the end
With the bottles around her
Alcohol and pills that will deaden her pain
And she has no regrets
That her life will be over
Because inside she died a long time ago

Alone in the grave
With no one to miss her
No flowers to show that somebody loved her
And nobody bothered
To turn up at the funeral
As alone in death as she had been in life

Sarah J. Vinnels 2004

Confidentiality

An excellent publication on Confidentiality is the publication of the Children's Legal Centre at Essex University – "Working with Young People".

If an adult talks with a young person that adult has a **duty of confidence** where the information has been agreed or notified it is confidential. I may well hear the young person giving the same information to another but still choose to treat what I have heard as confidential. However, before that discussion takes place with those under sixteen, parental permission must be obtained (only one parent's consent is necessary) unless the adult believes the under sixteen year old is competent. Competence is referred to in law for this age group as **Gillick Competence** – dealing with the child's understanding of their own actions' consequences. It would be taking risks to assume that those under 13 could be Gillick Competent.

Therefore **Good Practice** would be to involve the parents as much as possible – they may later withdraw their consent though I have never known that to happen. In work at schools I strongly invite senior students, even those who have reached eighteen, to inform their parents that they are seeing the school counsellor. The school's CPO must be informed wherever the issue is even a "maybe" child protection issue. As always I would inform the child what I proposed to do. In other words **absolute confidentiality** cannot be offered; health, well-being and life must take precedence. All the boundaries need to be spelled out at the beginning of the relationship.

Conditions of Worth Questionnaire

Please answer each question "Yes", "No" or "To some extent".

1. Do you set yourself high standards and then criticise yourself for failing to meet them?
2. Is it important to you to be right?
3. Do you feel discomforted (e.g. annoyed, irritated) by small messes or discrepancies
4. such as a spot on a garment or the wall paper, an ornament or a tool out of place,
5. a disorderly presentation of work?
6. Do you hate to be interrupted?
7. Do you like to explain things in detail and precisely?
8. Do you do things (especially for others) that you don't really want to?
9. Is it important to you to be *liked*?
10. Are you fairly easily persuaded?
11. Do you dislike being different?
12. Do you dislike conflict?
13. Do you have a tendency to do lots of things simultaneously?
14. Would you describe yourself as "quick" and find yourself getting impatient with others?
15. Do you tend to talk at the same time as others, or finish their sentences for them?
16. Do you like to "get on with the job" rather than talk about it?
17. Do you set unrealistic time limits (especially too short)?
18. Do you hide or control your feelings?
19. Are you reluctant to ask for help?
20. Do you tend to put (or find) yourself in the position of being depended upon?
21. Do you tend not to realize how tired, or hungry, or ill you are, but instead "keep going"?
22. Do you prefer to do things on your own?
23. Do you hate "giving up" or "giving in", always hoping that this time it will work?
24. Do you have a tendency to start things and not finish them?
25. Do you tend to compare yourself (or your performance) with others and feel inferior or superior accordingly?

Responses   (For scoring instructions see separate sheet)

	Yes	No	To some extent		Yes	No	To some extent
Q1				**Q6**			
Q2				**Q7**			
Q3				**Q8**			
Q4				**Q9**			
Q5				**Q10**			
Total				Total			

	Yes	No	To some extent		Yes	No	To some extent
Q11				**Q16**			
Q12				**Q17**			
Q13				**Q18**			
Q14				**Q19**			
Q15				**Q20**			
Total				Total			

	Yes	No	To some extent
Q21			
Q22			
Q23			
Q24			
Q25			
Total			

How to score the Conditions of Worth Questionnaire

1. For each question put a tick in one of the three columns "Yes", "No", and "To some extent".
   When you have finished the questionnaire, score your responses as follows.

2. For each of the five sections of five questions each, add up the number of ticks in each column, and write it at the bottom of the column. For each section, this should give you three figures totalling five.

3. For each section, take the total number of "Yes"es and multiply it by two. Add this result to the total number of "To some extent"s. The result of this addition gives you the total score for that section, which will lie in the range 0 to 10.

4. This score gives you a measure of the degree to which your behaviour is driven by the need to fulfil that particular condition of worth.

5. The conditions the various sections measure are as follows:

QQ 1 to 5: Be Perfect	QQ 6 to 10: Please others / Please me
QQ 11 to 15: Hurry up	QQ 16 to 20: Be strong
QQ 21 to 25: Try hard (...and don't succeed).	

Self-Awareness Diary sheet

Day.............................. Month........................ Year....................

Tick 3 boxes to indicate which were important to you today

☐ What did I feel?... Did I openly express that feeling? Yes/No Did others notice? Yes/No

☐ What did my body language say?..................................... Was it open or closed to others?.............................

☐ Did I talk to all the group members? Yes/No Do I remember their comments? Yes/No

☐ Was there something that I felt uncomfortable about? Yes/No How do I feel about and deal with silence in the group?.............................
....

☐ What change do I want in me?..
....

☐ What changes have I allowed myself to experience?..........................
....

☐ Any comments (on the above or other feelings)
....
....
....
....

Student Profile (Self-Assessed)

Scores 1 – 5 (degrees of involvement)

Name...

Date								
Process								
Break								
Theory								
Practice								
Self-awareness								
Awareness of Others								

Module 2

Checklist

Module content:	
	1. Reminder of group rules
	2. Process
	3. Checklist
	4. Any relevant and up-to-date material
	5. TA theory – a very brief introduction to the PAC diagram; Script Matrix......................
	6. Work on own Script Matrix
	7. Look at the significance of the exercise on Drivers of Module 1

Transactional Analysis

I introduce TA to course participants to illustrate from what Ego States (of students and staff) the behaviour, thoughts and feelings are originating. I am particularly aware of how appropriate TA (first developed by Eric Berne) can be when applied to the classroom situation. Alvin and Margaret Freed's "TA for Tots", "TA for Kids", "TA for Teens" are very useful when thinking of work in the classroom – both for staff and students.

The Drivers like "Be strong"; "Be perfect"; "Try hard"; "Please others" and "Hurry up" relate to the Script Matrix and to the work done on the "Conditions of Worth" questionnaire and it is useful to remind course participants to the antidote to the Drivers: "Be open and express your wish"; "You are good enough as you are"; "Do it"; "Please yourself"; "Take your time".

Ego States

The ITAA define TA as: "..a theory of personality and a systemic psychotherapy for personal growth and personal change" Eric Berne, the creator of TA, was a psychoanalyst and developed his EGO STATE model from his understanding of the Super-ego, Ego and Id – about FEELINGS, THOUGHTS and BEHAVIOURS copied from parent figures, responses to the here and now and replays from childhood. The diagram can be a template for both Structural and Functional analysis.

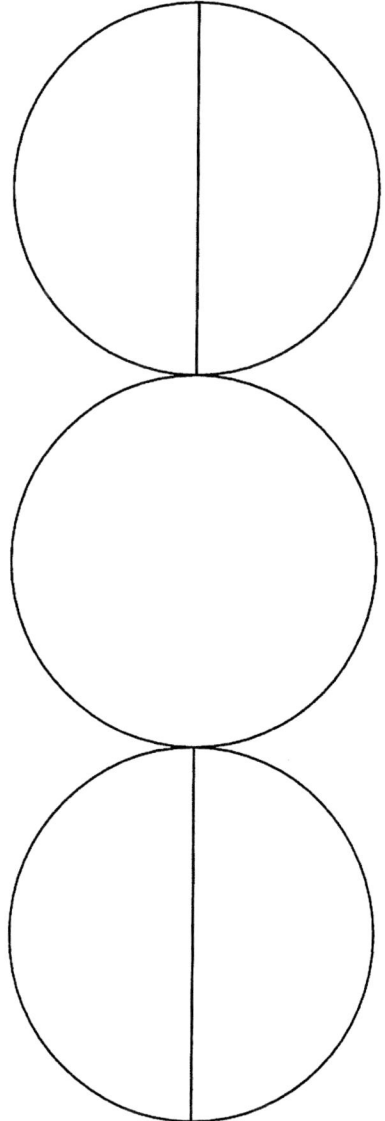

Structural Pathologies

The outlines can be used to illustrate pathologies like Symbiosis and Exclusion.

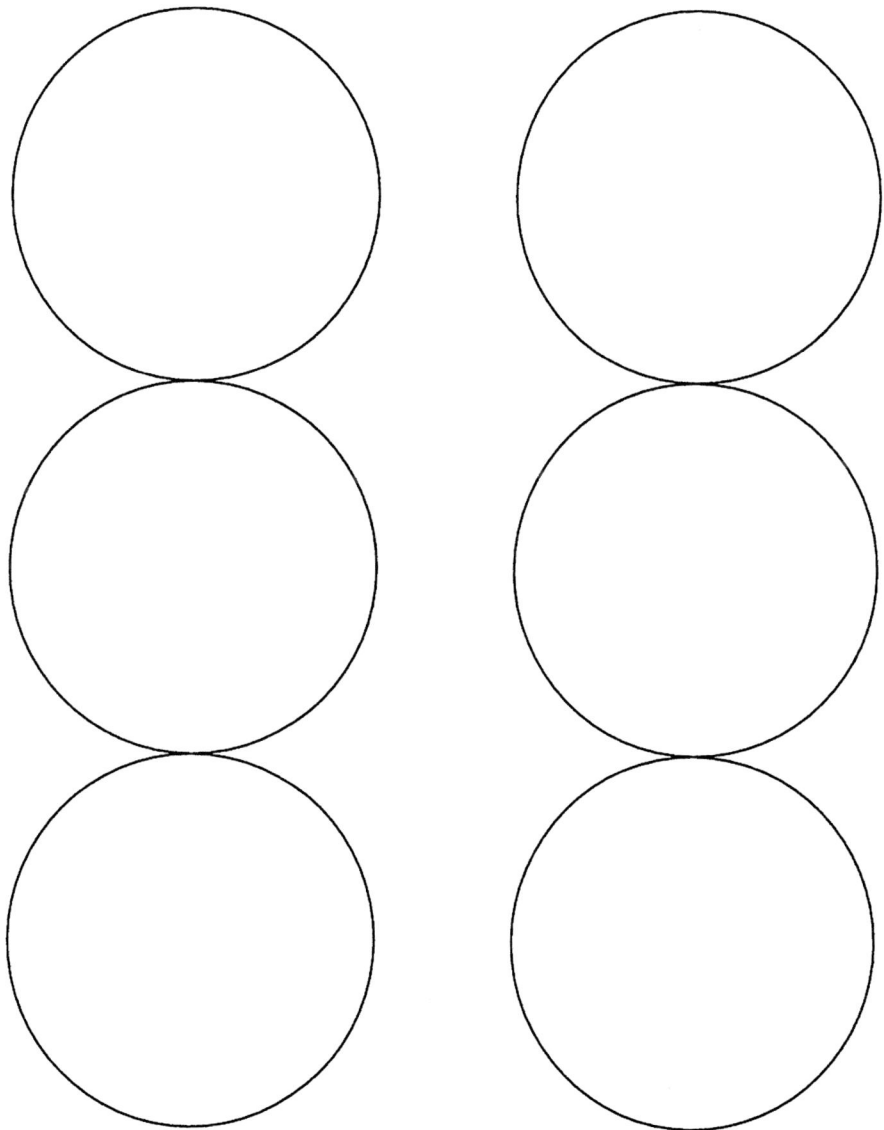

Script Matrix

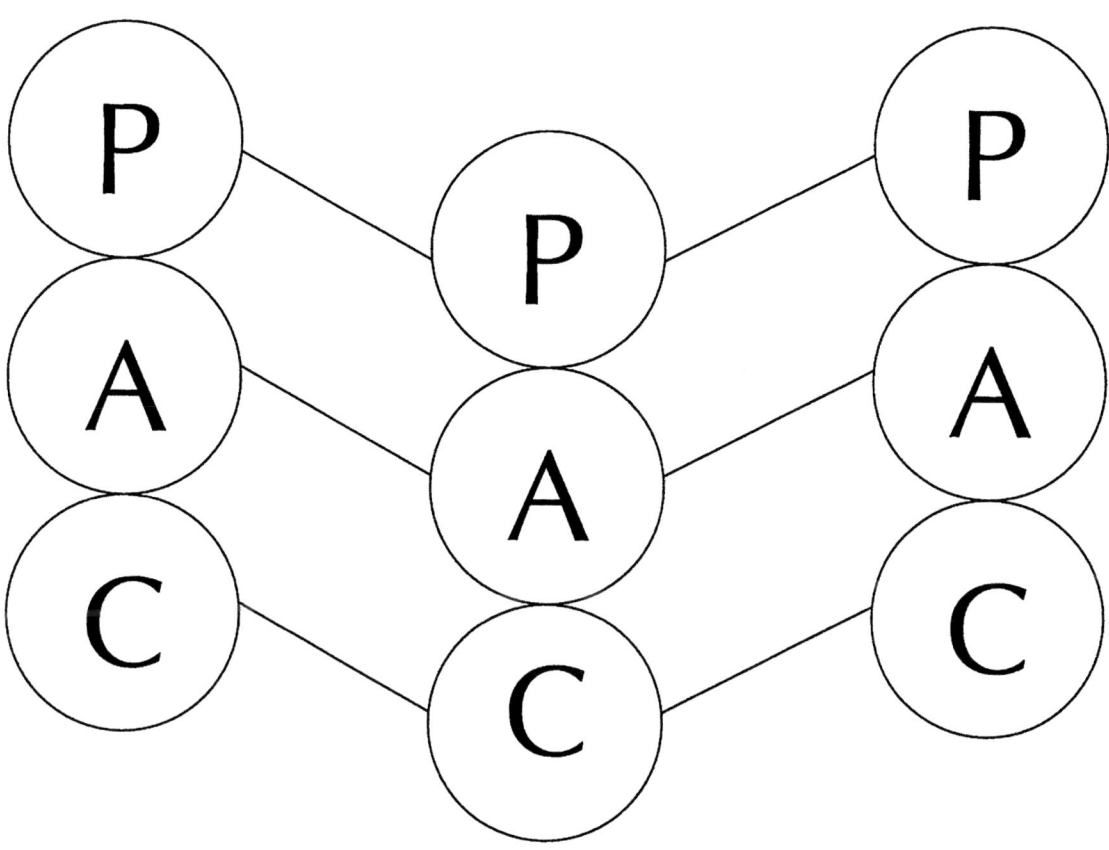

Taken from work of Claude Steiner

C. Steiner "Script and Counter-script TAB 5/18 1966 pages 133/135

Drivers

In module one there is a questionnaire called "Conditions of Worth" – it is an exercise considering what are called the "Drivers" in our life "Script" (see exercise on Script Matrix – TA theory).

These drivers can be called:
1. Be Perfect;
2. Be Strong;
3. Try Hard;
4. Please Others;
5. Hurry Up.

They can be identified with characteristic gestures, postures, facial expressions, words and tones.

To be most effective, competent and therefore finding enjoyment in our work and life we need to remove the compulsiveness of these Drivers that we have put into our life Script. In therapy a client can be shown alternatives or "Allowers" which they may be invited to consider.

So in place of the Drivers we can note that:
1. Being Perfect is not possible, so allow ourselves to be human;
2. We are all vulnerable and accepting that we can make our strengths less brittle.
3. We could allow ourselves some fun in our life and work.
4. Pleasing others is fine as long as we also please ourselves,
5. We may allow time for being creative and playful.

Behavioural Clues to Drivers

Driver	Words	Tones	Gestures	Postures	Facial Expression
Be Perfect	Phrases in parentheses Counts points off by numbers "As it were" "As we have seen" "That is to say"	Clipped Even Well modulated Precise enunciation	Counts on fingers Strokes chin "Steeples" finger-tips (V shape)	Upright Balanced round midline (resembles adult)	Eyes look upwards (less often downwards) and to one side, during pauses. Mouth slightly tensed, pulled out at corners
Be Strong	"Distancing" eg "You make me angry" "this bores me" "It feels good"	Flat Monotonous Usually low	Gestures few or absent	Immobile Closed (arms folded, legs crossed)	Immobile Expressionless
Try Hard	"Huh? Uh? What?" "I'll try to..." "I can't" "It's difficult" "Don't get you"	Tense Strangled Muffled Hesitant	Hand by side of head (as if straining to see or hear) Clenched fists	Strains forward Hunched-up	Screws up brow (two vertical lines above nose)
Please Others	"(high)...but...(low)" "OK? All right" "Kind of, sort of" "Hmmm?"	High Squeaky Rises at the end of a sentence	Head nodding Hands reaching out (usually palms up)	Shoulders hunched up and forward Leans toward other person	Looks up under raised eyebrows Crinkles brow into horizontal lines Exaggerated smile, teeth bared Turns face downward
Hurry Up	"Quick" "Must rush" "Let's go" "No time"	Staccato Machinegun-like Runs words together Fidgets	Taps fingers Wags foot Wriggles	Agitated changed of posture	Rapid, frequent shifts in gaze

Module 3

Checklist

Module content:	**1.** Process
	2. Checklist
	3. Demonstration counselling session
	4. Copies of blank Client Sheets used for Confidential records
	5. So which student needs counselling here? Discuss in pairs and then report back to the group
	6. Sample client analysis sheets – records of client numbers; f/m; year and classes of referees; presenting issues...........................
	7. Drama and Beneficial Triangles

Counselling Demonstration

Think about the dialogue and the body language and what is not said.
At the end of the session the counsellor will debrief the client (necessary whether client's own material or a role play).

Then any comments you have must be directed to the counsellor ONLY. Those comments may be about:

1. How you felt as an observer
2. How the counsellor responses to the client by both her body language or her comments
3. How you expected it to be?
4. Do you think this is a long term piece of work or could it be suitable for brief therapy?
5. ....

Analysing a Counselling Session (in groups)

1. What do you think was the issue the Client wanted to talk about?

2. Did their **body language** say anything different?

3. Did the counsellor show any of the following qualities?

   - Empathy
   - Congruence
   - Unconditional positive regard

4. In the words of Transactional Analysis what Ego State did the Client show and how? What Ego State did the Counsellor show and how? Remember the P/A/C diagram.

5. What might you have done differently?

Which Student/s Need/s Counselling?

Client Assessment Sheet (school)

Name:...

Male/Female...............................

Age............... School Year................. Form...........................

Address:..

....

Referred by:..

Parental Consent:...

Family/Place in family:..

....

Important others:...

Religion:..

Medical History:..

....

Earlier Therapy/counselling:..

Date and Time:..

Client Story:..

....

....

....

Client Pro Forma

Client no.............. Date and time:...

Recording Yes/No.....................

Appearance...

New issue/continuation...

....

Feelings: Client...

....

　　　　　　Counsellor...

....

Process...

....

....

Content...

....

....

Closure...

....

....

Next session...

Client Analysis

Towards the end of the Academic Year I submit a statistical analysis of clients seen to my Line Manager (number of students seen, years from which they came, issues brought (issues brought may differ from an underlying issue), levels of attendance. I additionally keep a diary of sessions, which remains nearly as confidential as my notes as it contains my record of client names. An attendance record must, of course, go to the Year Head each day of clients I see and I update the lesson register (nowadays easily done by computer) — it is not possible to keep absolute confidentiality of client names in a school.

The analysis sheet would contain information like:

2003/2004 — to date (say early June, when exams reduce client load and permit such an exercise)

Year 7: 9 clients referred	Year 11: 7
Year 8: 10	Year 12: 15
Year 9: 9	Year 13: 5....
Year 10: 8	

It is also valuable to indicate numbers of boys and girls in such a list, though I find it is usually quite balanced by gender. I sometimes find myself with a majority of older students and need to consider if this is a product of spending 20+ years of my teaching with post-16 students. In other words this exercise is important for me as well as valuable information for senior management.

Issues brought: I put these in order of greatest (possible) presentation. Again I warn that these may differ significantly from the underlying issue, which may take some time to emerge.

1. Cross-cultural family difficulties — especially girls.
2. Self-image
3. Family break-up
4. Bullying
5. Bereavement
6. Sexual
7. Medical (client or family member)
8. Parenting
9. Depression..... and many others

These of course will vary significantly with the make-up of the school population. The list is valuable feedback for referring staff and teachers to be more aware of.

Beneficial and Drama Triangles

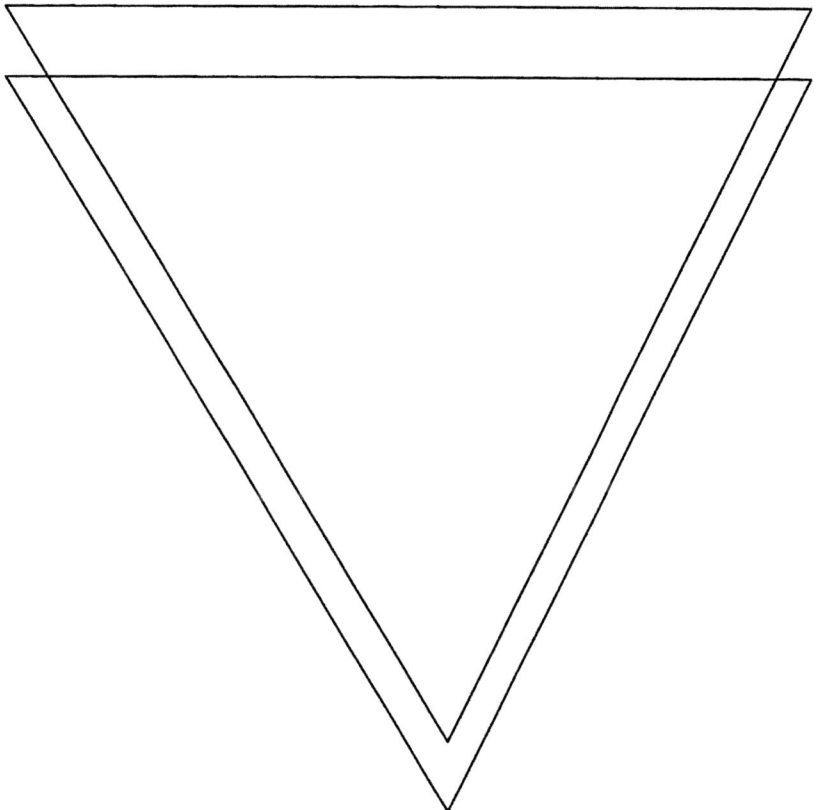

Module 4

Checklist

Module content:		
	1.	Process
	2.	Checklist
	3.	Questionnaire on Multiple Intelligence
	4.	List of Multiple Intelligences
	5.	Definition and Principles of Emotional Literacy
	6.	Skills analysis
	7.	Application to work at school

Multiple Intelligences

Definition:

The ability to solve problems or to create products that are valued within one or more cultural settings.

Howard Gardner, 1993

1. Verbal – Linguistic

2. Mathematical – Logical

3. Spatial

4. Bodily – Kinaestic

5. Musical

6. Interpersonal

7. Intrapersonal

8. Naturalist

You and Your Multiple Intelligence Profile

Linguistic	
Books are important to me.	
I hear words in my head before read, speak, or write.	
I get more out of listening to the radio or a cassette than watching a video or the TV.	
I have aptitude for games like scrabble, anagrams, and passwords.	
I enjoy tongue twisters, puns etc.	
I am sometimes asked to explain the meaning of words.	
English, social studies, and history are easier for me than maths and science.	
I pay more attention to words on adverts as I travel through the town centre than buildings or environment.	
Conversation often refers to things I have heard or read.	
I have written something recently or spoke on a subject that received good attention.	
TOTAL	/10

Logical mathematical	
I can compute numbers in my head.	
I play games and teasers that involve logical deduction or sequencing.	
I like to set up little experiments – if I double the amount of plant food I give what will be the result.	
My mind searches for patterns, regularities, logical sequences in things.	
I am interested in new developments in science.	
I believe that most things have a have rational explanation.	
I think in wordless, abstract concepts, often without images to go with them.	
I find logical flaws in things other people have said or done.	
I feel more comfortable once things have been measured, categorised, analysed, and quantified in some way	
TOTAL	/9

© Elizabeth Morris, School of Emotional Literacy

Spatial	
I see clear visual images when I close my eyes.	
I like using a camera or camcorder to record what is going on.	
I enjoy jigsaws, mosaics, mazes and other visual puzzles.	
I have vivid dreams quite often.	
I can generally find my way around unfamiliar territory.	
I like to draw or doodle.	
I find geometry easier than algebra.	
I can easily imagine how something would look if seen from a birds eye perspective.	
I like looking at reading matter that is heavily illustrated.	
TOTAL	/9

Musical	
I have a pleasant talking voice.	
I can tell when a note is off key.	
I frequently listen to music on the radio, cassette etc.	
I play a musical instrument.	
My life would be poorer without sounds and rhythm around.	
I find myself walking around with a TV jingle or tune running through my head.	
I can easily keep time clapping or tapping to a piece of music.	
I know tunes to a lot of different songs or pieces.	
If I hear a rhythm/song/musical piece I can reproduce it fairly accurately.	
I often make little tapping routines or hums while working, studying or learning something new.	
TOTAL	/10

Bodily kinaesthetic	
I engage in some sport activity regularly.	
I find it difficult to sit still for long periods of time.	
I like working at concrete activities with my hands eg weaving, sewing, modelling, mechanics.	
My best ideas come when involved in some physical activity – walking, jogging, swimming.	
I frequently use hand gestures when conversing with others.	
I need to touch things to learn more about them.	
I enjoy dare-devil amusement rides or thrilling physical challenges.	
I would describe myself as well coordinated.	
I need to practice new skills rather than see them demonstrated.	
TOTAL	/9

Intrapersonal	
I regularly spend time reflecting, thinking, meditating, wondering about important life questions.	
I have attended counselling or personal growth sessions of some sort to learn more about myself.	
I read self help books for the same reason.	
I have my own opinions.	
I have a special interest or hobby that I keep private.	
I have important goals for my life that I think about on a regular basis.	
I have a realistic view of myself that I have found out through feedback and reflection.	
I would rather be in a quiet cabin in the woods than a busy entertaining resort.	
I am often considered to be strong willed/independent minded.	
I often keep a journal to keep me in touch with the events of me inner life, such as my dreams and my emotional responses to places and people.	
I am self employed or very autonomous in work or have thought a lot about starting my own business.	
TOTAL	/11

Interpersonal	
People come to me for advice or suggestions about their situation.	
I prefer team sports to individual ones such as swimming.	
I like to talk problems through rather than mull over them alone.	
I have at least three close friends.	
I like games like Monopoly, Bridge rather than Crosswords or individual computer games.	
I like to teach someone else what I know how to do.	
I am often considered as the leader in a group.	
I feel comfortable in a crowd.	
I like to get involved in community/social activities.	
I would rather spend an evening at a lively social gathering than at home alone.	
TOTAL	/10

© Elizabeth Morris, School of Emotional Literacy

Naturalist Intelligence	
I have always enjoyed the outdoors.	
I have hobbies such as hiking, fishing, rock climbing.	
I am very conscious of smells and natural sounds where-ever I go.	
I regularly retreat to natural spaces to revitalise.	
I have got green fingers.	
I always had a pet or an ongoing relationship with some animals.	
I collect or collected minerals, flowers, insects etc (and often still have these collections)	
I am comfortable rooting around in mulch or 'yucky' material when exploring.	
I am very good at spotting even the smallest detail.	
I feel an affinity for the natural world.	
I get excited about a flower coming into bloom or the return of the swallows.	
TOTAL	/11

Complete totals on the histogram over the page.

© Elizabeth Morris, School of Emotional Literacy

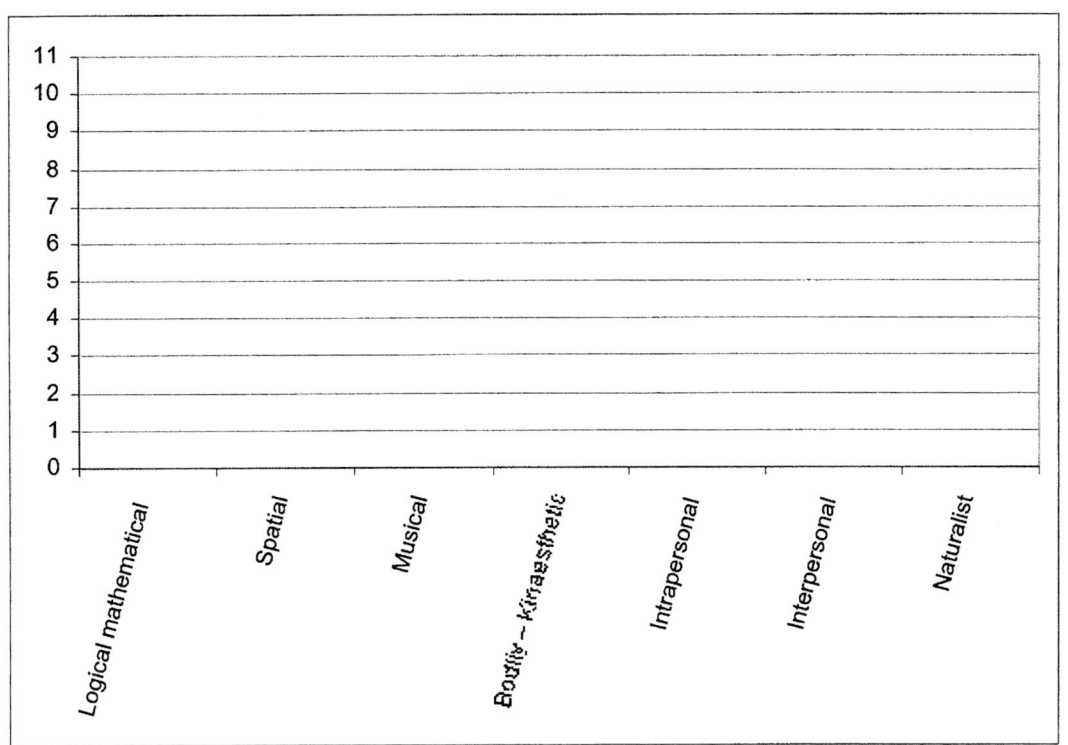

What does this mean about how you teach?

_____

_____

_____

Think of a lesson plan that you were planning to use this week and do the Multiple Intelligence test on it.

Now turn to the Action plan page and make some notes or mind maps for yourself as you plan the next steps to integrating multiple intelligences into your classroom

© Elizabeth Morris, School of Emotional Literacy

Emotional Literacy – Case Study

My co-trainer, Heather Daulphin, leads the module on Emotional Literacy and Multiple Intelligences, and in her inimitable style relates it brilliantly to the school's experience and needs. It takes the following format in outline.

"Overview
The introduction of EL is part of the strategic development to strengthen the pastoral support in Hampstead School. At the heart of this work is the notion that good emotional health is central to the students' educational success. There were three strands in the school's work to strengthen the pastoral support for the students at the school.

1. The Pastoral curriculum.
We believe that the pastoral curriculum should be systematic, rigorous, age appropriate, and support students' personal and emotional development so that they become effective students who feel positive and confident about themselves, have high personal aspirations and who have developed the capacity to be reflective, empathic and respectful young adults.

2. Clear systems, structures and policies to encourage/facilitate personal development and safeguard emotional well-being.
Here we wanted to go beyond policies such as anti-bullying, equal opportunities and exclusions, and consciously establish structures to encourage students to take responsibility for their behaviour. School councils, classroom codes and peer mentoring are but a few. Such democracy works in tandem with school support services such as Mentors, Counsellors and Learning Support Units.

3. A Commitment to ensure that all staff have the necessary mentoring skills to work effectively with students.
All teaching staff should have the mentoring skills and be as concerned for the students' emotional maturity as their academic development. This would suggest that the teacher who has strong interpersonal skills and is more empathic is more effective. The emotionally literate teacher is central to this strategy. We believe that the possession of emotional competencies as well as good subject knowledge and an understanding of effective pedagogy are essential for all teachers in schools."

(The passage in quotes is an extract from the published article of Heather Daulphin, in the Journal of the National Association of Head Teachers, June 2003)

Having introduced the school's overview to emotional literacy the group can then be invited to define emotional literacy, to think about the qualities they might require in order to be emotionally literate and to think about the key principles from which this concept stems. Then they can be handed sheets with Elizabeth Morris' definition and her list of principles. Then, because the school had a cohort who undertook the Certificate in Emotional Literacy Development Course from the School of Emotional Literacy, it is possible to look at the impact upon those teachers on the course, in their work (and likely their personal lives as well). This information was then tabulated under the following headings. I do not set out the whole table, but rather the headings, as it includes the staff names and details of changes particular to Hampstead School.

Individual Projects (a requirement of the Certificate Course)

Course member	Focus	Target	Group	EL competency/ principle	Activity	Impact

An extraordinary percentage of the students listed have published their findings and gained significant personal promotion.

Emotional Literacy

Definition:

"Recognising, understanding, handling and appropriately expressing emotion in ourselves and other people".

Dr. Elizabeth Morris, Principal, School of Emotional Literacy.

Principles:

1. We are each of us in control of, and responsible for, our actions.

2. No-one else can control our feelings.

3. People are different – in experience, feelings and wants.

4. However you, and they, are is OK (not necessarily what you do).

5. Feelings and behaviour are separate. (In the therapy world we look at and invite changes in Feelings, Behaviour and Thinking)

6. All feelings are justified, acceptable and important.

7. Change is possible.

8. PHYSIS – all people have a natural tendency towards growth and health.

Emotional Literacy – Skills Analysis

Adapted from the work of Dr. Elizabeth Morris

Groups of Skills:
1. Self- awareness
2. Self-management
3. Awareness of others
4. Managing others

Individual Skills:
1. (a) Reflection
   (b) Body awareness
   (c) Problem solving
   (d) Decision making

2. (a) Heart Smart
   (b) Anchoring
   (c) Verbalising feelings
   (d) Energy management
   (e) Mood management
   (f) Asking for what wants
   (g) Knowing body signals
   (h) Goal setting
   (i) Anger management
   (j) Stress resilience
   (k) Self-talk
   (l) Impulse control

3. (a) Empathy
   (b) Body-language – literate/openness/tolerance
   (c) Risk evaluation and trusting regard for others

4. (a) Negotiation
   (b) Mediation
   (c) Respectful concentration
   (d) Apologising and making amends
   (e) Conflict handling
   (f) Giving feedback
   (g) Complimenting
   (h) Toleration of differences
   (i) Resisting pressure – emotional blackmail

Module 5

Checklist

Module content:	**1.** Process
	2. Checklist
	3. Human Brain
	4. Stages of Group Membership
	5. Group Diagrams
	6. What needs to happen in groups?

The Triune Brain

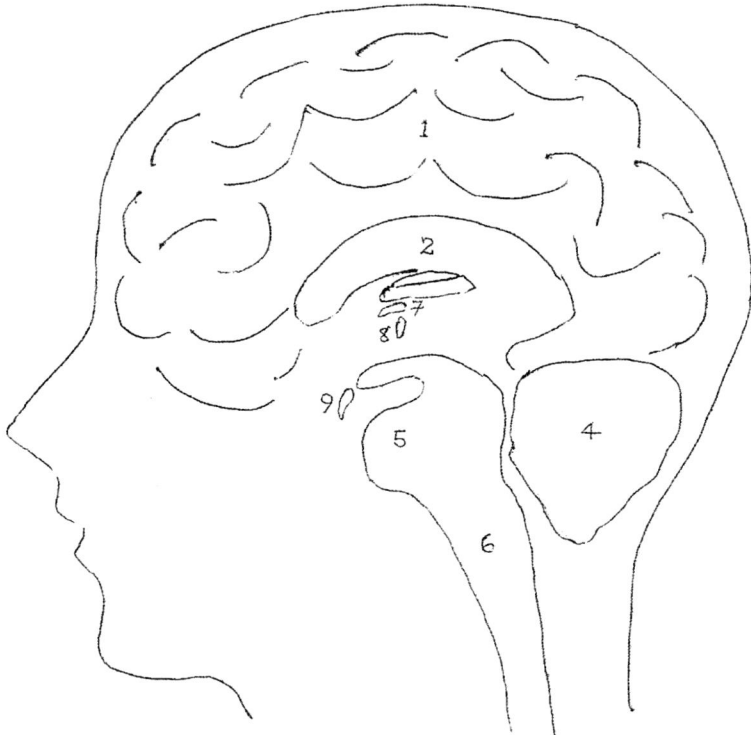

The Triune Brain: Basal Ganglia, Limbic System, Neo-cortex – the three areas of the brain upon which recent research has shown the impact of adrenaline, cortisol and dopamine upon our states of feeling.

The areas indicated above include:
1 = Cerebral Cortex (seat of all intelligent behaviour) + 2 Corpus Callosum = Cerebrum (responsible for initiation and co-ordination of all voluntary activity in the body ad governing the functions of lower parts of the nervous system); 4 Cerebellum (maintains muscle tone, balance and sychronisation of activity in groups of muscles under voluntary control – no initiation or intelligence); 5 Pons Variollo + 6 Medulla Oblongata (autonomic activity like heart and lungs); 7 = Thalamus, 8 Hypothalamus; Pituitary Body.

Recent Brain Research

In addition to looking at the different areas of the brain and what recent research tells us about the workings of the brain, it is useful to be able to point course participants to fuller articles where they may follow this up.

In an interview article of the BACP journal of November 2004 there is an excellent review of such a piece of research – the interview arising from Sue Gerhardt's new book "Why Love Matters: how affection shapes a baby's brain": I hope this glimpse may encourage researching the article or book.

Sarah (interviewer): "And the prefrontal cortex is the part of the brain that plays a major part in managing our emotional lives?"

Sue (Gerhardt): "Yes, it's the part of the brain that enables us to empathise …. What most people don't realise is that we are not born with the capacity to empathise"

She goes on to point out that with neglect in the early moths of life, the prefrontal cortex development will be minimal and she cites studies of murderers and the Romanian orphans seen recently on our TV screens. There have also been studies done on the impact of dopamine (the feel – good hormone) upon our capacity to work.

The stages of group membership

From the three main "schools" of TA, the Classical school pays particular attention to Group Process. There has thus developed a picture of five stages to group process;

- Pre-Forming

- Storming

- Norming

- Performing

- Adjorning

It is a useful exercise for the group to run through how they felt about considering taking part in this course to how they feel breaking up on completion of the course.

In 1965 Tuckman set out what he considered to be an analysis of these stages (see next page). Course participants may want to take further a brief introduction to this work by referring further to Tuckman's work.

Stages of Group/Team Life

Stages of group / team life	Common issues	Emotions	Leader's focus	Leader's tasks/attitude	Leader's issues
Pre-stage 1 (Shellott et al., 1958) *Pre-forming*	(For individuals) joining, commitment	Ambivalence unwillingness	On preparation	To inform, explain and prepare	Type of leadership
Forming	Attachment/ Structure	Resistance/ Interest			
Norming	Ambivalence/ Dominance	Enthusiasm/ Reluctance			
Storming	Intragroup Conflict/ Challenge	Anger/ Anxiety			
Performing	Resolution/ Withdrawal	Interest/ Motivation			
Adjourning	Clarifying/ Recycling	Sadness/ Relief or Excitement			

© Tuckman 1965

Group Structure

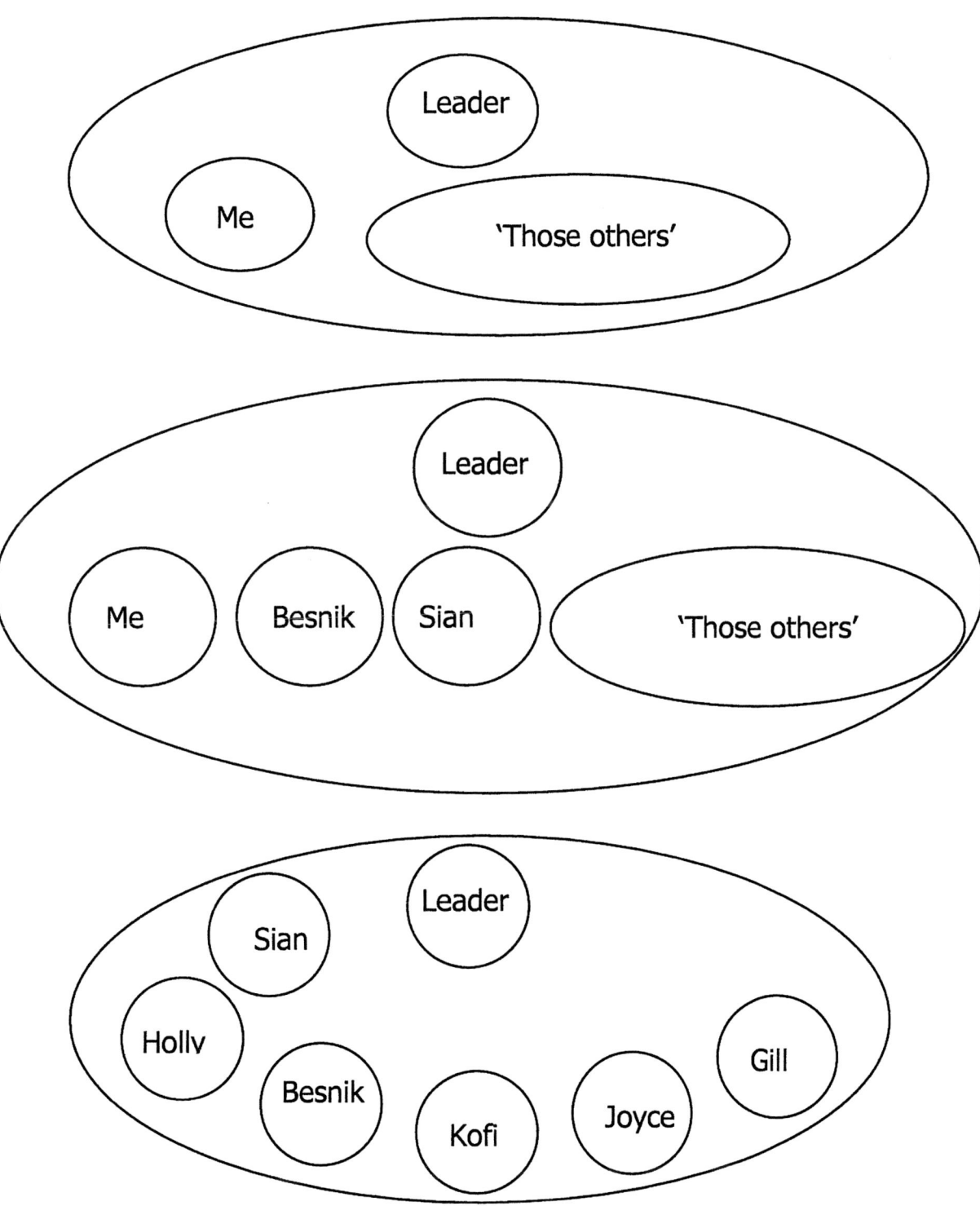

What needs to happen in groups?

- Emotional engagement

- Meaningful encounters between people

- Change in attitude

- Emotional, Social and Academic Learning

Module 6

Checklist

Module content:	**1.** Process
	2. Checklist
	3. The Core Conditions of Carl Rogers
	4. Rogers stages of Growth
	5. Demonstration counselling session
	6. Statement for delivery at final session

Statement for Delivery at Final (Goodbye) Session

You may want to prepare a readable statement or simply use it for your thinking. Remember it is OK not to make a statement.

Does anything stay clearly in your mind from the course?

Did you learn anything that invited personal change in you?

Did you learn anything that invites you to bring change to the way you work with you students?

Is there anything you wish to say to a colleague before this group is disbanded?

Person Centred Counselling

Carl Rogers' necessary and sufficient conditions (from a paper in 1959)

"For therapy to occur it is necessary that these conditions exist:

1. that two persons are in CONTACT;
2. that the first person (the Client) is in a state of INCONGRUENCE, being VULNERABLE or ANXIOUS;
3. that the second person (the Therapist) is CONGRUENT in the relationship;
4. that the therapist is experiencing UNCONDITIONAL POSITIVE REGARD towards the client;
5. that the therapist is experiencing an EMPATHIC understanding of the client's frame of reference;
6. that the client PERCEIVES, at least to a minimal degree, conditions 4 and 5."

These six conditions are well explained in "Person Centred Counselling in Action" by Mearns and Thorne, Sage 1988.

They are brought up to date by Keith Tudor, "The case of the lost conditions" BACP Journal 11/1 (February 2000)

Carl Rogers' 7 Stages of Growth

In 1961 Carl Rogers wrote "On Becoming a Person" he noted various changes in clients, through therapy, with a series of indicators of change. These can be looked at as "The 7 Stages of Growth" – or they could be expressed as 7 levels of feeling:

1. Stage one sees the client not recognising problems or feelings.

2. The client can describe or talk about feeling in the past but does not own them.

3. Feelings are described rather than felt – as though unacceptable.

4. A standard kind of client comment could be "well one would feel angry" suggesting non-responsibility for (anger).

5. Free expression of feeling in the present.

6. A flow of feelings – an immediacy which Rogers saw as "dramatic".

7. Appropriate expression of feelings such that the client can handle this stage without the counsellor.

Peer Buddying Course Analysis of a Counselling Demonstration

1. What did the body language of the client say to you?

....

2. What did the body language of the counsellor say to you?

....

3. Was there much eye contact between the client and counsellor?

....

4. What did the client say was the presenting issue?

....

5. Do you believe that was the underlying issue?

....

6. In TA language what ego state did the client appear to be showing?

....

7. How did the counsellor demonstrate the qualities of empathy, congruence and unconditional positive regard?

....

8. Is there any question you have for the counsellor?

....

9. How comfortable would you have been with that client?

....

Module 7

Checklist

Module content:

1. Process	

2. Checklist

3. An Egogram

4. OK Corrall/Phenomenology

5. Review of earlier modules
  - i. Reminder of poem – do you see it differently now?
  - ii. Significance of Confidentiality
  - iii. Ask yourself about your diary sheets
  - iv. TA approach
  - v. Which student needs counselling here?
  - vi. Drama and Beneficial Triangles
  - vii. Emotional Literacy
  - viii. Multiple Intelligences
  - ix. Counselling demonstrations
  - x. Brain research
  - xi. Group theory
  - xii. Personal Centred approach

Have you prepared your paragraph for the last module?

Egogram

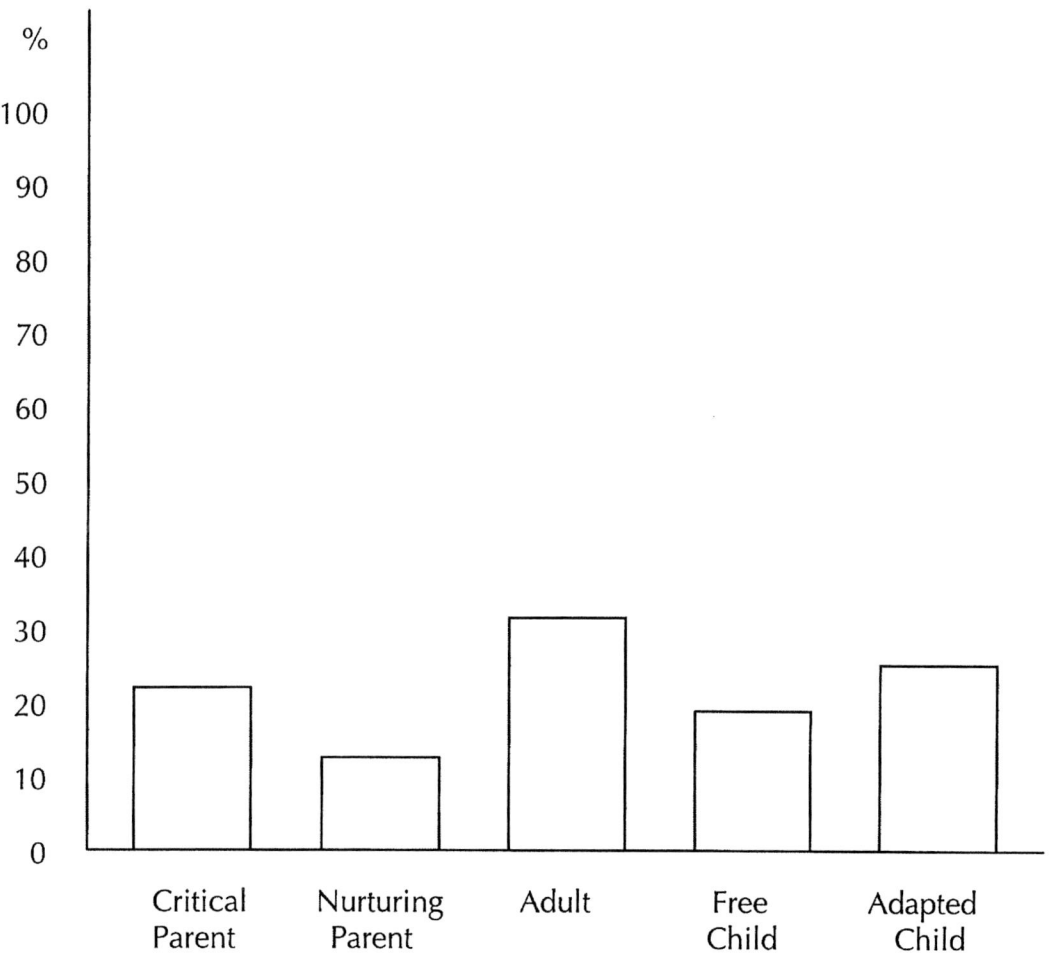

Taken from work of Jack Dusay

The OK Corral

YOU-ARE-OK

Depressive wanting to Get Away From	Healthy position wanting to Get On With
Futile position, Client cannot Get Anywhere With	Position of paranoia where Client wants to Get Rid Of (others)

I-AM-NOT-OK (left) I-AM-OK (right)

YOU-ARE-NOT-OK

When Franklin Ernst developed this piece of work it was to explain "what is happening" for the client and we can apply the model of thinking to explain for ourselves our own and students' feeling, thinking and behaving.

The model can be taken further by plotting how we feel at a series of times and thereby plot a scatter diagram and a best-fit picture. This enables us to see how close or far that is from the healthiest quadrant of the OK Corrall. This takes us further than Berne's process of script formation and the conviction of the OK'ness/not OK'ness.

Franklin Ernst: "The OK Corrall: the grid for get-on-with" TA Journal ¼ 1971 (pages 231/240).

A People Place

Is this not a place where tears are understood,
Where do I go to cry?
If this is not a place where my spirits can take wing,
Where do I go to fly?
If this is not a place where my questions can be asked,
Where do I go to seek?
If this is not a place where my feelings can be hears,
Where do I go to speak?
If this is not a place where you'll accept me as I am,
Where can I go to be?
If this is not a place where I can try to learn and grow,
Where can I just be me?

William J Crocker

Module 8

Checklist

Module content:	
	1. Process
	2. Checklist
	3. Gloria video
	4. Where would you place this in the OK Corrall?
	5. Paragraph deliveries and responses
	6. Sources and further reading
	7. Evaluation sheets
	8. Certificates of attendance

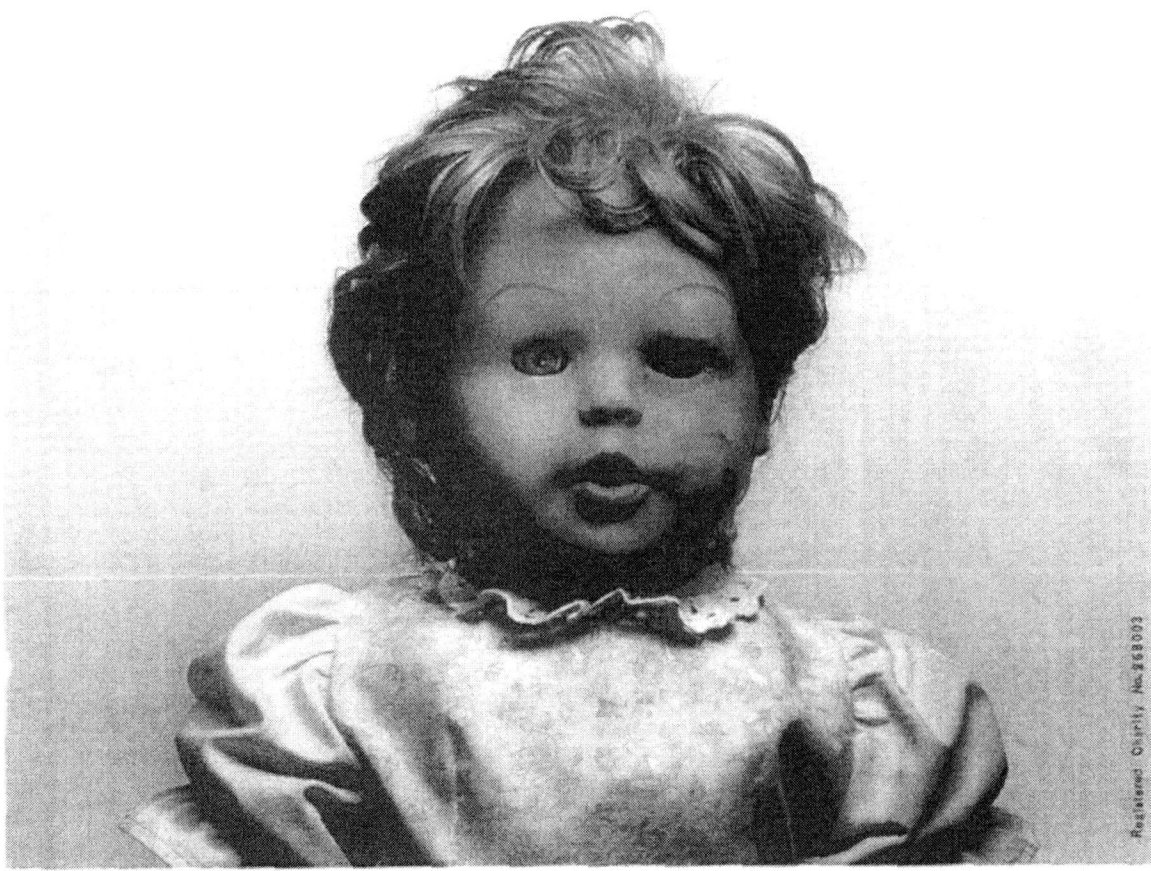

Jessica Safar lives in Bethlehem,
a place still affected by conflict.

Three years ago, while out with
her family, she was hit by shrapnel
that tore out her left eye.
Her physical wounds could be
treated, but her mental scarring
was even more severe.

She had given up hope. Hope of ever
having a normal life with a career,
a husband and a family.

In desperation she gouged out
the eye of her doll, hoping that
it would become more like her.
Someone to share her pain.

Counsellors funded by Christian Aid
have been helping Jessica come
to terms with what has happened.

Giving her practical advice and
helping her to realise she can
still lead a fulfilling life.
As well as just listening.

Inspired by Jessica's story,
Christian Aid has launched the
'Child of Bethlehem appeal'.

This Christmas, millions of people
affected by war and poverty
desperately need your support.
Just £30 could pay for counselling
for three children unnecessarily
injured by conflict in the Middle East

Please ring now on 08080 006 006 or
go to www.christianaid.org.uk/christmas
to make your donation.

What kind of child does this to her doll?

Reproduced by the kind permission of Christian Aid

References and Reading List

1. Nurturing Emotional Literacy by Peter Sharp 2001, David Fulton Publishing

2. Emotional Intelligence by Daniel Goleman, Bloomsbury Publishing 1996

3. Mental, Emotional and Social Health: A Whole School Approach by Katherine Weare, 2000

4. Establishing a Counselling Service in your School by Emma Wills, School of Emotional Literacy Publishing 2003

5. Working with Young People by Carolyn Hamilton, The Children's Legal Centre at Essex University

6. Person Centred Counselling in Action, by Mearns and Thorne, Sage Publishing 1998

7. TA Today by Stewart and Joines, Lifespace 1987

8. TA for Kids (also for Tots and for Teens) by A and M Freed 1977

9. Post Graduate level Certificate and Diploma in Emotional Literacy Development Course (Masters Course available soon) available from The School of Emotional Literacy, email info@schoolofemotional-literacy.com or visit www.schoolofemotional-literacy.com

Emotional Literacy and Counselling Skills

Course Evaluation

Please complete and return

SECTION A
Please **circle** the appropriate rating for questions **1/3**
Rating: 1.Very Good   2.Good   3.Satisfactory   4.Poor

1. How do you rate the course content?	1 2 3 4
2. How do you rate the material provided?	1 2 3 4
3. How do you rate the methods of delivery?	1 2 3 4

SECTION B
Please **circle** the appropriate rating for questions **4/6**
Rating for question 4: 1.OK   2.Too long   3.Too short

4. Was the course the appropriate number of sessions?

    1   2   3

5. Was there a best module for you? Y/N - if Y.....

    1   2   3   4   5   6   7   8

6. Was there a least helpful module for you? Y/N - if Y...

    1   2   3   4   5   6   7   8

SECTION C
Please be fuller in your answers to questions **7/8** (overleaf if necessary)

7. Do you have suggestions for inclusion/exclusion for further such courses?

8. Any other comments (especially in relation to the course relevance to your work)?

Thanks.

Emotional Literacy and Counselling Skills - Introductory Course

.... SCHOOL

Certificate of Attendance

This is to certify that .... has attended

this course with course leader ....

eight modules of fortnightly sessions from

....

....

Course Leader Name   **Signature**

....

Date of certification

What Next for the Counsellor and School?

When you have been working with school staff in the arena of Emotional Literacy and in the arena of Feedback from staff handling challenging or worrying behaviour, it is possible to gain intelligence of their thinking about what has helped and what might help in further initiatives. Thus I now have feedback from clients' teachers, tutors and Year Heads; feedback from Peer Buddies involved with students who turn to them for Buddying; I have feedback from Peer Buddies about their training; I have feedback directly from clients who come to see me and I have feedback from staff who take part in the Introductory Course set out in this Workbook.

What I am saying is that working as a counsellor in an institution like a school has a very different component from working as a private practitioner in the confines and isolation of a private consulting room. For me it professionally extremely important as it offers me an additional perspective upon thinking about Boundaries and Advice when working with young people as opposed to the adult majority of my private clientele. This I learn both from the response of the student clients (an age group that I have worked with all my professional life) and from the feedback of all those listed above. Out of this feedback also emerge new ideas.

Soon I hope to consolidate upon my work with the Peer Buddies and especially to learn from the innovation of last year. We responded to a request from last year's Peer Buddy trainees when they asked for more training beyond the set modules. The Youth Worker, who kindly helped me to deliver the course last year, suggested a Residential Weekend as a way of both responding to the request and a creative way of enhancing the training. It was a phenomenally successful experience which both honed the Peer Buddies Buddying skills and also formed them into a truly cohesive team. It also gave Leila and me, together with two other colleagues, a much better understanding of how to deliver training and to learn from the act of training.

A further initiative which I suggested to the school last year picks up wonderfully on the work with the Peer Buddies: Supervision. Buddies working with other students must, of course, have supervision of their work. Last year I felt that in an emotionally literate school, Supervision should be offered to staff, probably a pilot group, say Year Heads, to begin with. That idea is now before the Senior Management Team for consideration.

School of Emotional Literacy

Since we started publishing in 2003 we have grown our library to over 30 publications, all of which have been written and designed by practitioners for practitioners. All our titles have been tried, tested and adjusted before going into print so that we are able to offer the very best tools to help you: tools which we know work, which are practical and which are readily accessible to any one who wants to help children fulfil their potential. We are always expanding our publications range because we are continually developing new resources to meet the demands of practitioners and to incorporate the latest research findings.

We can happily keep you up to date about new title releases by adding you to our mailing list, or you can browse our shop online at www.schoolofemotional-literacy.com where you can see everything we have on offer to help you.

If you visit our website you will see that our publications are not the only way in which we could support you. Our mission has always been to create the best chance for every child through the provision of a positive emotional education. From being the first organisation to bring materials for assessing emotional intelligence to Europe, more than 10 years on we now work in different countries across the world to support and train all the adults, whether they have a professional or a personal relationship, who work with children. We firmly believe that by developing children's emotional intelligence you ensure that they are more likely to be able to reach their potential in the widest sense, helping them to become well-rounded, creative, academically able, happy and socially adept people at the end of their schooling.

We offer training in a variety of forms to suit your individual needs, such as:

- Accredited Post-Graduate level Certificate, Diploma and Master's in Emotional Literacy Development
- Workshop days related to the practical applications of emotional literacy development, self-esteem building, supporting SEAL, behaviour management... and many more
- Train the Trainer courses in peer support, restorative practices and transforming relationships
- Conferences on all aspects of emotional literacy development

Above all, we are specialised consultants, experts in tailoring our services to suit our individual clients' needs. Being this flexible allows us to offer very effective recommendations to ensure maximum impact and sustainability.

If you would like more information on any of our services, then please feel free to give us a call or look at our website.

Other Publications

1. The Whole School Emotional Literacy Indicator by Elizabeth Morris and Caroline Scott
2. The Class Emotional Literacy Indicator by Elizabeth Morris and Caroline Scott
3. The Individual Emotional Literacy Indicator by Elizabeth Morris and Caroline Scott
4. Developing Social Skills – A Practical Solution by Elizabeth Scott
5. Build Self-Esteem First – A Practical Solution by Athy Demitriades
6. Establishing a Counselling Service in your School – A Practical Solution by Emma Wills
7. I feel.... when..... Posters developed by Elizabeth Morris
8. Graffiti Feelings Posters by Claire McAleavy
9. Bullies aren't bad. An emotionally literate response to bullying by Heather Jenkins
10. 'SISTERS' Club Facilitators File by Annie Hamlaoui
11. Emotional Resilience Profile by Elizabeth Morris
12. Self Esteem Guidelines: developing a whole school policy by Elizabeth Morris
13. Face your Feelings Game by Liz Tew and James Bocot
14. Feelings Game by Heather Jenkins
15. IT'S OKAY TO BE ME by Annie Hamlaoui
16. The School and it's Counselling Service - a companion guide to "Establishing a Counselling Service in Your School - A Practical Guide" by Emma Wills
17. Multiple Intelligences in the Classroom: At-a-glance Guide to Assessing and Teaching using Multiple Intelligence Theory by Elizabeth Morris
18. EL Indicator for Early Years by Elizabeth Morris and Caroline Scott

OBR www.incentiveplus.co.uk or call 01908 526120